YOUR DREAM JOB

How to Land the Job of Your Dreams

Write a Brilliant CV

JO BANKS

Published by What Next? Media – sales@whatnextconsultancy.co.uk

For Sharon...

Thanks for being there!

"The best way to predict the future

is to create it."

Abraham Lincoln

Contents

Foreword.. vii

Freebies..xi

Introduction... xiii

Why Should You Use This Programme?......................... xiii

The 'Your Dream Job' Programme.......................................xiv

Book 1 – Managing Job Loss....................................xiv

Book 2 – Finding Your Dream Job...................................xiv

Book 3 – Write a Brilliant CV.....................................xv

Book 4 – Foolproof Interview Skills...................................xv

Book 5 – Managing Job Offers..................................xvi

What You Will Learn In This Book...xvii

Chapter 1 – Writing a Brilliant CV 1

Why CV's Get Rejected..2

Using Power Words..7

Write In The Third Person 10

Chapter 2 - The CV Structure... 13

Section 1 – Heading..14

Section 2 – Summary Statement 15

Do Not Use Opinion...17

Avoid Using Clichés..18

Summary Statement Examples.................................19

Section 2 - Key Skills.................................20

Key Skills Exercise.................................21

Section 4 - Career History.................................24

Section 5 - Qualifications & Training.................................38

Section 6 - Additional Information.................................40

Top Tips for Completing your CV.................................46

Chapter 3 - Covering Letters.................................49

Chapter 4 - Application Forms.................................53

What Next?.................................61

Keeping Up Momentum.................................61

Frequently Asked Questions.................................64

Additional Resources.................................69

Your Dream Job Online.................................71

What's Included In This Programme?.................................72

Write a Brilliant CV.................................72

Finding Your Dream Job.................................73

Foolproof Interview Skills.................................73

What Next Online School.................................74

Reference Links.................................75

About the Author.................................77

Connect With Jo.................................81

'Thoughts Become Things'.................................83

Foreword

"Passion is the difference between having a job and a career."

Welcome to Book 3 in the *'Your Dream Job'* series. This programme has been designed specifically to give you all the tools, techniques and support you need to land Your Dream Job. It covers everything from successfully managing job loss, getting clear about your next role, effective CV writing and, foolproof interview skills, to how to handle the all-important job offer and everything else in between.

Following from the success of my second book, *'Land Your Dream Job Now!'* I received feedback suggesting that it would be useful for readers to be able to purchase individual sections, specific to their needs, e.g. CV Writing, Interview Skills, etc. Thereby, making it more cost effective.

With that in mind, I have taken the original 'Dream Job' book and broken it down into individual sections, each addressing a particular topic within the job search process. This has allowed me the opportunity to revise the original content and add additional information that didn't make the original edit.

HOW AM I QUALIFIED TO WRITE THIS BOOK?

I set up my own business, What Next Consultancy (UK) Ltd in 2009. Since then I've personally coached over 1500 people with over 4,500 having attended 'What Next' Career Management Workshops. I personally work with clients to provide them with the tools, techniques and mindset adjustments necessary to identify what exactly it is they want, how/where to find it and how to go about getting it. Whether that entails a sideways move, promotion, or change of career, I help pave the way. I'm also proud to say that I've helped an ever-increasing number of clients start their own businesses.

Before setting up What Next, my background was in senior human resource management (HR), with a career spanning almost 20 years. During that time, I interviewed thousands of candidates ranging from forklift truck drivers to senior executives and CEOs. Having such an extensive background in recruitment enables me to instinctively know what companies are looking for during the selection process. It allows me to help my clients maximise their self-promotion, providing them with top tips that will put them ahead of their competitors, enabling them to land their dream job. It's often the small things that make a big difference.

Outplacement & Redeployment

At What Next, outplacement and redeployment programmes form part of our core offering. We provide both off-the-shelf and bespoke career management training to private and public sector organisations in the course of their ongoing commitment to their employees during change programmes, i.e. company restructures.

These courses include CV writing, interview skills, job hunting, presentation skills, together with how to start a business. We also offer one to one career management coaching sessions for more senior managers or those employees who are finding the transition particularly difficult.

One-To-One Sessions

Depending on the organisation's budget and the individual's needs, a dedicated coach will work closely with the job seeker on a one-to-one basis covering the following areas:

- Assisting them in getting clear about exactly the type of job they want, the kind of company they want to work for, the industry, role content and remuneration, etc.
- Recognising their transferable skills.
- Producing an outstanding, achievement-based CV – which can be written by the coach (depending on budget).
- Devising a bespoke step-by-step job search project plan.
- Identifying and contacting prospective employers on the client's behalf.
- Bespoke interview preparation, explicitly tailored to individual roles.
- Researching the interviewing company, providing the client with a full report containing pertinent information for use in the interview.
- Reviewing the interview feedback.
- Helping manage negative emotions, e.g. interview nerves etc., as well as maintaining motivation at optimum levels.
- Managing the job offer process including negotiating the remuneration package.

- Acting as a general sounding board as well as providing motivation.

- Support during the first 90 days in post.

We offer a comprehensive service, and although we do employ underlying principles, we tailor our programmes directly to the needs of our clients. Having that flexibility allows us to provide practical guidance that gets results.

We continually review our content using feedback from our delegates, clients, and associates; we also incorporate key trends and advice gained from our extensive contacts within the recruitment industry. These include close links with recruitment consultants, internal recruiters, professional recruitment assessors and HR professionals. This feedback enables us to remain up-to-date, reflecting the current recruitment landscape.

It's that information and knowledge that I've included in this book. It contains the very best, up-to-date information available... I can, therefore, say with authority that **this stuff works!**

FREEBIES

As an additional 'thank you' for purchasing this book, there are free resources available, designed to complement the learning described in this programme.

Visit **yourdreamjob.co.uk** and sign up with a quality email address to receive regular updates and an assortment of useful tools and information designed specifically to help *you land 'Your Dream Job'*.

Signing up will ensure that you are added to our exclusive group of like-minded individuals, who wish to learn the top tips and techniques to enhance their job search and get the edge over their competitors. Head over to the website and sign up now!

yourdreamjob.co.uk

There is also a dedicated Facebook group which you are welcome to join:

facebook.com/YDJYourDreamJob/

Introduction

"If it doesn't challenge you, it won't change you."

Why Should You Use This Programme?

Since the last recession which started in 2008/2009, the face of recruitment has changed significantly. Recruiters had to rethink their strategies to find low-cost options that would deliver quality candidates. As a result, the recruitment industry had to react quickly in response to the changing needs of its clients.

This programme includes practical, simple, down to earth advice that if followed step by step, will give you all the tools you need to gain a competitive advantage in a post-recession world. This information has been proven to work consistently with thousands of job hunters. It is practically foolproof when applied as described.

The information I've included in this programme works, no matter what level you work at, what job you're looking for or whether you're currently in or out of work; the principles and activities are the same.

It is intentionally written in a simple, uncomplicated language with a common-sense approach that you'll find it easy to follow and implement.

THE 'YOUR DREAM JOB' PROGRAMME

Within the 'Your Dream Job' programme, there are five individual books covering everything you need to know to land Your Dream Job. Following is a summary of each book and what it contains:

BOOK 1 – MANAGING JOB LOSS

- Facing Redundancy/Job Loss
- Managing Your Thoughts and Emotions
- Understanding the Change Curve
- Top Tips
- Taking Positive Action
- Frequently Asked Questions

BOOK 2 – FINDING YOUR DREAM JOB

- Get Clear – Establish What You Want/Don't Want from Your Next Role
- Managing Your Social Media
- Conducting An Effective Job Search
    - Online Job Sites

- o Job Centre Plus
- o Newspapers/Professional Journals
- o Recruitment Consultancies/Agencies
- o Head-hunters
- o Speculative Applications
- o Using LinkedIn
- o Networking
- o Planning your Job Search
- o Daily Activity Plan
- Frequently Asked Questions

Book 3 – Write a Brilliant CV

- Why CVs Get Rejected
- Appropriate CV Language
- CV Structure
- CVs for Students
- Covering Letters
- Application Forms
- Top Tips
- Frequently Asked Questions

Book 4 – Foolproof Interview Skills

- Overview of Assessment Types
- Online Testing
- Video Assessments
- Personal/Supporting Statements

- Situational Judgement Tests
- Telephone Interviews
- Skype Interviews
- How to Prepare for An Interview
- Using the S.T.A.R. Format
- Competency Based Interviews
- Top 10 Most Frequently Asked Questions
- Your Questions
- Second Interviews
- Assessment Centres
- Presentation Skills
- On the Day
  - Personal Presentation
  - Communication and Rapport Building
  - What to Take with You
  - Managing Nerves
  - After the Interview
- Frequently Asked Questions

BOOK 5 – MANAGING JOB OFFERS

- Negotiating the Terms
- The Paperwork
- References
- Making the Right Choice
- Resigning from Your Current Employer
- What to Do If You Get a Counter Offer

- What to Do If a Job Offer Gets Retracted
- Know Your Rights
- What to Do If You Change Your Mind
- Frequently Asked Questions

What You Will Learn In This Book

Book 3 in the 'Your Dream Job' series, provides all the information you need to Write a Brilliant CV. With so much competition in the marketplace, your CV has to stand out; it's no longer acceptable to regurgitate your job description. A CV is your primary marketing tool, and it is, therefore, essential to get it right.

In this book, I explain how to Write a Brilliant CV; what to include and more importantly what shouldn't be there. Not only will I provide you with a simple but effective CV structure, explaining how to complete each section in detail, I also supply you with numerous hints and tips to ensure that your CV stands out (in the right way) from your competitors.

Summary

I have helped thousands of people find the right job using the tools, techniques, hints and tips provided in the full Your Dream Job programme. To get the best results, I recommend using all the steps exactly as described.

Don't shy away from activities because they seem too hard, especially if they make you feel uncomfortable. Typically, they will be where you *should* be placing your focus. I also recommend creating a structured plan that you stick to and regularly review, ticking items off as you complete them. By doing this, you're more likely to achieve results, ultimately landing Your Dream Job.

NOTE - You will notice that I often repeat certain phrases or ideas throughout the programme. I make no apologies for this, as I consider these things to be critical aspects of job hunting, and, after all, *repetition is the mother of skill!*

CHAPTER 1 – WRITING A BRILLIANT CV

"If opportunity doesn't knock, build a door."

The majority of people I work with have never had any formal training on how to write a CV, and if they have, it was before the last recession. In fact, many don't even have one because they've been in the same role/company for a long time. For many, they have the same CV that they wrote when they first entered the job market. Subsequently, they have added job after job, without giving much thought to removing old, out of date information; resulting in an unwieldy, unfocused load of waffle!

Occasionally, when I'm delivering career management workshops to a corporate client, they will tell me that some of their employees have opted out of attending because they have 'a friend in HR' or a management colleague who has looked over their CV and, therefore, they don't need any help. They don't need it, of course, until they get the feedback from their co-workers about what I cover! Many managers, including HR professionals, can be terribly out of date when it comes to the requirements of a CV in today's competitive job market.

It's no longer enough to uplift your job description and insert it into your CV, which is unfortunately what most people still do. That's just sloppy and lazy and will not give you a competitive advantage. CV's these days have to be **ACHIEVEMENT FOCUSED**.

WHY CV'S GET REJECTED

Companies discard CVs for many reasons:

1. THEY AREN'T TAILORED TO THE VACANCY AND CONTAIN IRRELEVANT INFORMATION

   This is the overriding reason why CVs get rejected. If you include information that isn't relevant to the job you're applying for, you're wasting valuable space. Your CV is a marketing tool and should be used to provide as much evidence as possible demonstrating to the recruiter why you are suitable for that role. It should include your transferable skills, experience, achievements and qualifications.

   If it contains too much irrelevant information, it's not likely to get you past the pre-sift stage; the recruiter won't be able to see how your skills and experience match their criteria. You should avoid trying to list everything you've ever done; you just don't have space, and as your career progresses, it's likely that some information becomes irrelevant as it's replaced with more up to date skills, experience and achievements. Therefore, it's of the utmost importance that you only include information that's pertinent to the role for which you're applying.

Many clients struggle with this; they want to incorporate everything they've ever done because they think it looks impressive. On the contrary, if a recruiter can't see immediately, **on the first page**, how you match with their essential requirements, it's likely that your application will be rejected. Any additional information, i.e. anything that's not essential to the role, should be saved for discussion at the interview.

If there is more than one type of position that you would like to apply for, each requiring slightly different skills/ experience, there are two options:

i.   Write one extended CV, containing all your skills, experience, and qualifications (this could end up being four pages long). Each time you apply for a new role, edit the CV down to 2-2.5

sheets of A4 reflecting the skills/ experience required for that particular vacancy.

ii.   Create more than one CV, tailored to different roles, e.g. I recently worked with a client who had general management and project management experience. He didn't mind which position he ended up with, so we wrote two CVs containing specific skills and expertise pertinent to each of those individual jobs.

An excellent example to illustrate the importance of tailoring your CV was provided by one of my clients, who to be made redundant from his role of mailroom manager within a large corporation. When we had our initial one-to-one meeting, he told me that he'd been applying for supermarket management positions, as that was his previous career. He was upset because he had applied for forty vacancies, but hadn't had one interview. He couldn't understand why that was, because he had the skills and experience, albeit a few years earlier.

When I reviewed his CV, which was five pages long, it wasn't until the third page that I found his supermarket management experience. It was easy to imagine why he'd been passed over for an interview;

it wasn't immediately apparent where his skills and experience matched.

We re-wrote his CV putting his relevant experience on the first page, and he immediately started applying for more supermarket management vacancies. Within three days he had two interviews and was offered both jobs with the same week. That's the power of a 'tailored' CV.

NOTE - Recruiters are busy people. They will not search to see how you fit their criteria; you have to put it right on the first page so that they can see it straight away.

2. THEY ARE TOO LONG OR TOO BORING

Your CV should be no longer than two sides of A4 paper (two and a half at the very most if you have an abundance of qualifications). I often hear cries of horror when I tell delegates this in CV workshops. They think that they can't possibly reduce their whole career down to two pages. However, if a 55-year-old CEO of a large multi-national corporation can, you can! The key is to be selective about what you write, only including relevant information that reflects the requirements of the role(s) for which you are applying.

3. THEY ARE POORLY PRESENTED/ HAVE A POOR LAYOUT (TYPOS/ FONT/ PAPER/ PRINT, ETC.)

When I tell clients that their CV must be no longer than two pages, occasionally I'll be presented with two pages of tiny type font, with the margins pushed out to the very edge of the pages. **That's not acceptable.** CV's should be easy on the eye, with good spacing, using the right type font and size and plenty of white space. I recommend using typeface Arial pt 10 or 11 or Calibri pt 11 (do not use Times Roman, it's old-fashioned and will make you look outdated), with NO typos, spelling mistakes or errors of any kind.

It's tough to see our own mistakes, so you should get someone who has a good command of written English to proofread it, checking for errors including spelling and grammar. Using a CV that is full of spelling and grammatical errors is unacceptable, it is likely to be rejected no matter how excellent your skills and experience may be. I also recommend using a program like grammarly.com/, which you can either download or upload your documents to (Mac). Grammarly checks your spelling and grammar, and also makes suggestions to improve your English. I use it for all my writing and highly recommend it.

If you're printing your CV (I always advise taking three printed copies to each interview), make sure you use a more substantial weighted paper, don't just use cheap flimsy photocopy paper. Using good quality paper will tell the interviewer that you are professional and pay attention to detail. Also, make sure that copies are in pristine condition with no folds and no ragged edges – staples or paper clips are fine. The presentation of your CV is paramount.

4. THEY ARRIVE TOO LATE

Don't think that you can just sneak an application in after the closing date. The deadline is there for a reason, and you miss it, that indicates to the prospective employer that you can't hit deadlines – it's as simple as that. If, however, you find the job at the very last minute, i.e. just before the deadline, it may be worth contacting the recruiter to see if they will accept a late application. It's unlikely, but worth a try.

USING POWER WORDS

You can use power words to supercharge your applications. As you only have a limited amount of space on a CV, frequently you can replace three or four smaller words with one quality power word.

Following is a list of Power Words. Sign up at *yourdreamjob.co.uk* to receive a copy of this list along with other useful tools straight to your inbox.

Accelerated	Excellent	Persuaded
Accomplished	Expanded	Planned
Administered	Facilitated	Presented
Analysed	Financed	Processed
Approved	Forecast	Produced
Budgeted	Formulated	Programmed
Built	Founded	Promoted
Completed	Generated	Proposed
Conceived	Headed	Purchased
Conducted	Identified	Recruited
Consolidated	Implemented	Redesigned
Controlled	Improved	Reduced
Converted	Improvised	Reorganised
Convinced	Increased	Researched
Coordinated	Influenced	Resolved
Created	Initiated	Revised
Cut	Innovated	Set-up
Delegated	Installed	Simplified
Delivered	Introduced	Started
Demonstrated	Invented	Streamlined
Designed	Launched	Strengthened
Developed	Led	Stretched
Devised	Maintained	Structured

Directed	Managed	Succeeded
Doubled	Modified	Summarised
Earned	Motivated	Supervised
Edited	Negotiated	Trained
Eliminated	Operated	Transformed
Established	Organised	Utilised
Evaluated	Originated	

Keep a copy of the full list with you while you're writing your CV, covering letters and applications as it will help you to eliminate repetitiveness. Using power words expands your vocabulary making your written documentation look more professional than it may otherwise be.

Occasionally, I do get clients who say, *"But my CV doesn't sound like me! Shouldn't my personality come through a bit more?"* In short, no! **The sole purpose of a CV is to get you an interview.** As I've said previously, it's a marketing tool, and you should use it as such. Your CV should be well written, factual, laid out well (easy on the eye with plenty of white space) and tailored to each vacancy. You have the opportunity to add a bit of personality in the covering letter.

WRITE IN THE THIRD PERSON

Before I start to talk about the CV structure, there is one crucial thing that I must cover:

You must write your CV in the third person.

What that means is that you **must not** include 'I', 'me', 'my', 'me', 'we', etc. and must not mention your name other than at the top of the CV, above your contact details. Writing in the *first* person will make your CV look outdated and unprofessional. This rule also goes for the 'Summary Statement' section at the top of the CV as well as your 'hobbies/ additional information' at the end. For some reason, people often write the majority of their CV in the third person and then convert to the first person for these two sections – that's wrong.

I usually get gasps of horror when I tell clients that they can't use 'I,' 'me,' 'my', etc., and some struggle transferring their CV from first to the third person. However, I have an easy solution; when you take the 'I,' 'me,' 'my' out of a sentence it usually still makes complete sense. For example, if you have a sentence that says, *'I designed a new process'* just remove the 'I' to read, *'Designed a new process.'*

When you have someone proofread your CV, tell them about the 'I', 'me', 'my' rule. Ask them to pick out any that you may have left in (I'll guarantee that there'll be at least one that you've missed if you wrote the original in the first person).

CHAPTER 2 - THE CV STRUCTURE

"The right CV can open many doors."

There is no right or wrong when it comes to CV structure; there are many different layouts available. However, the one I use has been proven to help people to get an interview literally thousands of times.

I recommend six different sections:

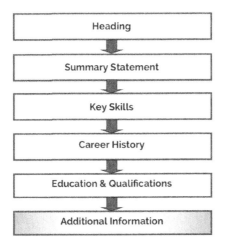

I realise that writing a CV, especially when you haven't done one for a while or if it's your first, can be daunting. Therefore, I've broken each section down, providing you with clear, concise guidelines as to what information to add in each.

Visit yourdreamjob.co.uk/ and sign up to receive a MSWord CV template which reflects the sections outlined here.

SECTION 1 – HEADING

Do Include:

- Name, location, email address and mobile phone number.

Don't Include:

- 'CURRICULUM VITAE' at the top of the page. Everyone knows what the document is. Therefore, writing the obvious is a complete waste of valuable space.

- 'Home' *and* 'mobile' numbers. Use the one a recruiter is most likely to get you on (usually your mobile). Many job seekers insist on putting their home number, and yet we rarely use them; leave it off – it isn't necessary.

Optional:

- Your home address. DO NOT INCLUDE IF YOU ARE PUTTING YOUR CV ON A JOB WEBSITE for data security reasons. You wouldn't put all of your personal information on a social media platform, so why would you put it on a website where anyone with a company can pay to have access to it? Instead, I suggest adding your location so that recruiters can see where you're located. Companies rarely write to your home address anymore; most correspondence is done over email, and, therefore, it's a waste of space to write this information on your CV.

SECTION 2 – SUMMARY STATEMENT

The 'Summary Statement' is the first thing that the recruiter reads and, therefore, it must clearly explain who you are and why you are suitable for the role. **This section MUST be tailored to the vacancy for which you are applying.**

In essence, the summary statement should consist of ONE PARAGRAPH, containing THREE POINTS:

1. WHAT ARE YOU?

    Your job title or something that reflects a generic title for the type of work you do. There can often be different job titles for the same role depending on the company. For example, HR Business Partner may be the same as a Head of HR or Senior HR Manager in other companies. If this is the case for you, I suggest using a generic title, e.g. 'Senior HR Professional'. If you do that, a recruiter won't get hung up on your job title, and reject your application because you don't have the same title or perceived seniority as that of the vacancy.

Another example of using a nonspecific job title is if you are seeking a general management position that requires standard management skills. In such circumstances, I would write 'experienced manager' rather than using a precise job title that may be only applicable to your company. You don't want to pigeon-hole yourself if there is more than one type of appropriate role that would be suitable.

However, if your job title *is* the same as the positions for which you are applying, for example, personal assistant, architect, accountant, general manager, etc. you would naturally use that.

2.   WHAT'S DIFFERENT ABOUT YOU?

In this sentence, write about what makes you different from your competitors. That could be your skills, time in the role, projects you've delivered, the size of the team or budget that you manage, anything that demonstrates your skills and the size of your job.

3. WHAT'S NEXT FOR YOU?

The type of role/ company/ culture you want in your next role. This sentence is optional, and some of my clients choose not to include it in favour of adding more information to 'what's different about you'. However, adding a sentence about what's next for you is an excellent way to tailor this section (see the examples later in this chapter).

DO NOT USE OPINION

DO NOT include things that the recruiter could perceive as subjective or just your opinion. Whatever you write must be factual and be backed up within your CV. Examples of what **NOT** to write are:

- Hardworking
- Trustworthy
- Dedicated
- Outgoing
- Team player
- Conscientious etc.
- Loyal
- Passionate

These words are nonsense in a CV context and a complete waste of valuable space. They are no more than your point of view, and for all the recruiter knows, you could have entirely made them up! However, one great word is 'experienced' as that definitely can be backed up within your CV.

AVOID USING CLICHÉS

I have to mention my pet-peeve here; please don't put *'Works well alone or as part of a team.'* Of course, you do! Who doesn't? Oh, my goodness, I hate that term, as do many recruiters. It is a complete waste of space on a CV and something that most people (for some reason) *think* they should include. It says nothing about you and is something that's just regurgitated rubbish which turns recruiters off.

Recruiters are looking for originality, and you want to stand out from the crowd, not be the same as every other applicant. I would estimate that at least eight out of ten people have that statement somewhere on their CV. Remember you only have limited space, so you need to use it wisely. Include facts that can be backed up, not nonsense statements that say nothing about you, your skills and experience.

SUMMARY STATEMENT EXAMPLES

The following are examples of what you might put in your 'Summary Statement':

EXAMPLE STATEMENT 1:

"(1) A qualified Prince2 Project Manager (2) with 15 year's experience in a variety of industries including logistics and manufacturing. With a proven track record of leading high performing multifunctional teams and managing continuous improvement. (3) Looking for the opportunity to utilise skills in a complex, multi-faceted change environment."

EXAMPLE STATEMENT 2:

"(1) An experienced Administrator (2) with an extensive background in building customer relationships, managing third party contractors and working within budgetary constraints. Possesses exceptional communication and organisational skills gained while working in a pressurised, customer focused environment. (3) Looking for the opportunity to develop existing skills and experience within a challenging environment."

Obviously, you won't put the (1), (2), and (3) in yours, I've just done that to demonstrate the three different parts, i.e.:

1. What you are
2. What's different about you
3. What's next for you

TOP TIP - Although this section is the first thing on your CV after the heading, it's often easier to write *after* you've completed the other parts. Therefore, you might want to write the next sections and then come back to your Summary Statement. Make sure that you do come back to it though – don't leave it out as it's a vital component of a Brilliant CV.

SECTION 2 - KEY SKILLS

The 'Key Skills' section is another part that you *must* tailor to the role. The easiest way to do this is to look at the 'essential' skills in the job advertisement, person specification or job description and list them in bullet point form (as long as you have those skills). You will demonstrate them later in the 'Career History' section.

Including the key skills using the recruiter's language is a little psychological trick designed to get you through the first pre-sift of applications. If you list your skills towards the top of your CV, it immediately tells the recruiter that you have what they're looking for, saving them valuable time and energy searching through your CV. They can see that you have the skills they require right up front.

Often, in larger companies, the pre-sift process is done via a computer program. The recruiter feeds a list of keywords into the program's search engine, and if it can find enough of those words in your CV, it will automatically go through to the next stage, if not, it will be rejected.

KEY SKILLS EXERCISE

In the absence of a job description/ person specification, make a list of your eight top skills and record them in bullet form. To help you with this, I've made a note of the most popular key skills collated from reviewing 100 typical job descriptions used by one of my large corporate clients:

- Administration

- Prioritisation

- Project Management

- Customer Service

- Managing Deadlines

- Report Writing

- Budget Management

- Influencing & Negotiation

- Relationship Management

- Problem Solving

- Networking

- Compliance

- Risk Management

- Strategy/ Vision

- Leadership

- Product knowledge

- Performance Management

- Planning & Organisation

- Communication

- Analytical

- People Management

- Risk Assessment

- Diary Management*

- Change Management

- Systems Knowledge

- Financial Management

- Stakeholder Management**

*Diary management means managing a diary for one or more people other yourself, e.g. a PA or secretary would list 'diary management' as a key skill.

** Stakeholder management is where you manage different contacts typically both internal and external to your business. Don't get this confused with networking which is something entirely different.

This list is not exhaustive. If you have a professional role, it's very likely that you'll have additional, specific skills related to your job, and, therefore, you should include those. My list is for guidance only, designed to get you started.

On your CV, you should list the bullets side by side in two columns. As you only have limited space, you can't afford to waste it by putting each skill on a new line. The easiest way to do this is to create a table, complete your list, then remove the table's lines.

This is how to display your key skills on your CV:

• Organisational Design	• Budget Management
• People Management	• Strategic Planning
• Negotiation	• Stakeholder Management
• Business Development	• Project Management

TOP TIPS - For writing your key skills.

1. The 'Key Skills' section is another part of your CV that you **must** tailor to the role for each application.

2. It's likely that you will have far more than eight essential skills, and you may wish to write more when you're first creating your CV. You can then take out any that aren't applicable when you're applying for a particular vacancy.

    NOTE - Your finished CV should only contain eight key skills, tailored to the vacancy for which you are applying.

3. If you have a job description/ person specification or job advertisement, match your skills to the 'essential' skills that the recruiter stipulates (provided that you have them).

4. List your key skills in a table format on your CV so that you have two per line. That way you aren't wasting valuable space.

SECTION 4 - CAREER HISTORY

This part of your CV demonstrates your job history, including your current and previous roles, and is where you have the opportunity to describe your skills and achievements. It's this section that shows the recruiter what they are 'buying' if they choose you.

Top Tip - This section must be *achievement focused*, i.e. **don't just regurgitate your job description; you must list your most significant accomplishments**.

I make no apologies for repeating myself here; gone are the days when you could copy and paste your job description. That's no longer acceptable and isn't likely to get you through a robust selection process. Recruiters now want to see your ACHIEVEMENTS, i.e. what you have done in your current and previous roles that have added value. If you write your accomplishments rather than endlessly listing your duties, it will undoubtedly put you ahead of the competition.

Structuring your Current and Previous Roles

Always start with your most recent/ current job first and then work backwards. For your current and past positions (if you've been in your current role less than ten years) use the following structure (I will discuss older posts later in this section):

1. A brief summary of the job, indicating size and scope

   • It's a good idea to include one line about your current/last company. Providing this information is of particular importance to management, and professional roles as it gives the recruiter an idea of the size of the organisation. Include facts such as the number of employees and locations, turnover, etc.

TOP TIP – Your company's website usually has at least one great sentence you could use for this purpose, typically found on the 'About Us' page.

- Explain what you're responsible for/ your *essential* duties. DON'T LIST EVERYTHING YOU DO, and DON'T USE BULLET POINTS. This section should be a *summary* and contain the most important aspects/ duties/ responsibilities of your role.

    For example, if you manage people, you don't need to list all the tasks involved such as timesheets, holidays, disciplinaries, grievances, performance management, etc., you should write 'managing a team of X' or 'people management' as everyone knows what managing a team involves.

- If 'administration' is part of your role, you don't need to write, photocopying, filing, typing reports, etc., again everyone knows what tasks it entails, just write 'administrative duties.'

- Include as many facts and figures as you can (especially for management/ professional/ executive roles), e.g. the number of people you manage, the size of your budget, the number of locations in your remit, your portfolio size, etc. This information shows the employer the size of your role.

- Top Tip – The summary should be no longer than one paragraph. It can be quite tight to get everything you need to in such a short space, and some clients can struggle with this. That is until I ask the question, *"What would you tell me that you do if I met you in the street? How would you explain the key responsibilities/ duties of your job to someone who doesn't know you?"*

  I appreciate that this can be difficult if, in the past, you wrote all of the critical tasks from your job description on your CV. Therefore, it may be helpful to think of what you say to people when they ask you what job you do. You may need to add a little more detail, but in essence, you won't go wrong if you follow this advice.

  You may want to look at your current job description as often the role summary or role purpose fits here. But, please **don't** start writing bullet points containing your responsibilities. That isn't what I'm suggesting, that's an outdated format that many people still use, but it won't help you to stand out from the crowd.

- Structure this paragraph in the following way:
  a. A sentence about the company including size, location, number of employees, etc. (See the 'About Us' page on your company's website.)
  b. *'Reporting to [job title] key responsibilities include* [write your key responsibilities].'
  c. *'Additional duties involve* [write any additional duties].
- Remember to keep this section relatively high level, i.e. don't add too much detail – this is NOT a regurgitation of your job description.

2. YOUR ACHIEVEMENTS

Your achievements are the most critical parts of CV as they are your chance to impress prospective employers and for them to see what they get if they choose you, i.e. what you can do for them. This section should include:

- **At least eight bullet points demonstrating your significant achievements** – By achievements I mean the things that you have delivered in your role that have added value to the business. I recognise that this is potentially a new concept for some; many delegates don't realise that they have any! However, we all do, no matter what job we have, otherwise there would be no point in having the role! People often find it difficult to think about what they've achieved, and when I start to coax it out of them, they'll often say, *"But that's just my job!"*

To be clear, YOUR ACHIEVEMENTS ARE THE RESULTS OR OUTCOMES OF YOUR ACTIVITIES/ DUTIES/ RESPONSIBILITIES.

To help remind yourself of what you've accomplished:

o **Ask your Manager** – They should be able to tell you.

o **Ask your colleagues** – It's likely that they have been part of the same activities or remember what you've been involved in.

o **Review your performance management/ job appraisals** - Most large companies have a formal appraisal process, and therefore, it is likely that your achievements will be in the documentation. If you don't have a copy of the paperwork, you can usually request it from your manager or HR department.

○ **Look back through your diary** - What meetings have you attended in the last couple of years? Quite often as soon as we finished a project or a piece of work, we completely forget about it and quickly become engrossed in the next. Looking back through your diary is an excellent way of reminding yourself of what you've been involved with and the achievements that came out of it.

• **Each bullet should show a business benefit** – If you don't have a management role, then you may find this a little tricky as often we don't always ask *why* we are doing something, we just do it! If you're unsure, ask your manager (if possible) or your colleagues.

• **Demonstrate different aspects of your role/ your key skills** – This is where you get the opportunity to demonstrate the skills that you mentioned in the second section. Each bullet should evidence a different ability if possible.

- **TAILOR YOUR ACHIEVEMENTS TO A SPECIFIC VACANCY** – One of the primary reasons for writing your achievements is for the recruiter to think, *'Wow, that's great. We want them to do 'that' for us!'* Therefore, tailoring your achievements is an essential way of showing that you can add value to a prospective employer.

- TOP TIP **- Explain each achievement in no more than two sentences** (these are bullet points, not paragraphs). The bullet point should contain two parts:

  o **What you did** – Succinctly explain what you did. Use your power words here, starting bullet points with verbs like Delivered, Negotiated, Designed, Implemented, Conducted, Completed, etc.

  o **What the outcome/ result was** – Include the business benefit, i.e. what the business gained by your achievement. Add as many facts and figures as you can here; if you don't know them or can't remember, go and find out! Numbers are always an eye-catcher. You should include percentages, cost savings £X, examples of where you've met/ exceeded budget and by how much, and the results of critical negotiations, KPI achievement (Key Performance Indicators) and targets met/ exceeded, etc.

TOP TIP – **Your achievements must meet the 'So What?' test** – If you can say, *"So what?"* after a bullet, then you haven't put in enough information. You need to drill down and think about why you did what you did and what the outcome/ benefit was to the business. I drive my clients mad with this one; I'll keep asking, *"So what?"* until we've established the absolute business benefit.

Here are some example achievements from actual client CVs:

- Successfully established and grew a design, manufacturing and retail company from an initial partnership to an organisation employing a workforce of over 40 people. Achieved year on year increase in turnover from £500,000-£750,000 within 12 months.

- Introduced a new appraisal process. Increasing employee completion from 38% to 92% within twelve months, enabling structured succession planning.

- Executive lead for a significant change programme incorporating the restructuring of teams and directorates, managing redundancies and recruitment processes. Delivered a structure which is fit for purpose enabling £1 million costs savings within three months.

- Delivered a new business improvement project over a six-month period. Resulting in increased capacity and cost savings in excess of £200k.

- Managed a large-scale IT recruitment project (60 specialist roles). Delivered on time and within budget.

- Planned and implemented £100k upgrades to communal heating systems. Achieved the most efficient option for each scheme, with no disruption to customers.

- Reviewed and redesigned the company's filing system, resulting in higher efficiency and substantial time savings.

- Successfully negotiated with suppliers regarding their pricing structures to reduce costs resulting in higher efficiency. Delivered cost savings of 5% on the previous year.

- Worked diligently, to continually meet and exceed KPIs of eighty picks per hour.

- Successfully managed the yearly 'Company Fun Day' which contributed to the achievement of the company's social charter.

PREVIOUS ROLES UNDER TEN YEARS OLD

For the role before your current or last one (if you're currently out of work), you should follow the same structure as described above but with fewer achievements, i.e. **a brief summary of the role showing size and scope, together with four to six key achievements.**

If the next previous position (three roles ago) is less than ten years old and is similar to the vacancies you are applying for now, then write the principal responsibilities/ purpose, but only include two-three achievements.

The nearer your previous positions are to being ten years old, the fewer achievements you need to add. That is unless one of those jobs is the same or similar to the type of vacancy you want to apply for now, but is different to what you have been doing for the last few years (see my 'mailroom manager' example from the 'Why CVs Get Rejected section). If that's the case, you should include six-eight achievements.

If you have had more than three roles in the last ten years, for those older jobs, you only need to write the 'summary' section and leave out the achievements altogether.

HOW TO WRITE OLDER ROLES

For jobs that are more than ten years old, it may not be appropriate to write as much information, especially if those roles have nothing to do with the types of positions you are applying for now. Therefore, write the **summary of the job showing the size and scope** as mentioned above. Again, unless vacancies you're applying for now, are similar to previous roles (again think about the 'mailroom manager' example), you don't need to include any achievements.

For roles that are over fifteen years old, you need only write the dates, the company, and your job title, as it's not likely that they have any bearing on the roles that you are applying for now.

For example:

Job Title - Company	**Date**
Job Title - Company	**Date**
Job Title - Company	**Date**

TOP TIP - Put the dates of your positions on the right-hand side. The reason for that is two-fold:

1. Sometimes recruiters can get hung up on how long you've been in a role. Putting dates on the right-hand side makes them stand out less, as we read from left to right. This advice is particularly useful if you've been in the same company for a long time as some prospective employers may think that you've been 'institutionalised' and, as a result, may believe that you will find it difficult to adjust to a new company or only know one way of doing things. Alternatively, if you've had a number of jobs in a short space of time, it could be considered that you have no 'staying power' and are likely to leave.

2. It gives you a few lines back. Remember space is at a premium with only two sides of A4; therefore, you can't afford to waste whole lines for just dates.

TOP TIP - Always check that your dates are correct. Writing incorrect dates is a typical error that many applicants make. Ensure that your dates from job to job run consecutively.

HOW FAR SHOULD YOU GO BACK WITH YOUR WORK HISTORY?

How far you go back on your CV is entirely up to you. The Equality Act 2010 makes it unlawful to discriminate against employees, job seekers, and trainees because of age, e.g. rejecting an applicant because they are 'younger' or 'older' than a relevant and comparable, existing employee. However, if you've been working for 30 years or more, you may not wish to highlight that fact to a prospective employer.

If that is the case, consider excluding jobs that you had in the first few years after leaving school/ higher education as it's likely that those roles don't relate to what you're doing now. For example, before I started my career in HR, I was a Personal Assistant to a Director of a large company. As my career in HR progressed, my previous PA role became irrelevant, and therefore, I removed it from my CV.

NOTE - Some organisations including banks, Police, Fire, HM Forces and some public sector companies may require your complete career history. However, it's likely that you'll need to complete an application form for those types of roles rather than a CV.

SECTION 5 - QUALIFICATIONS & TRAINING

In this section, you are going to list:

- Formal qualifications, e.g. degree(s), GCSEs, O Levels, A Levels, CSEs, etc.

- Formal, career-based qualifications, e.g. CIPD, ATT, CIMA, NEBOSH, etc.

- Work-based training (in-house courses) **undertaken less than five years ago** - anything older than five years will not be considered as relevant. For example, I once had a client who included an employment law seminar he attended six years ago – employment law changes every six months and, therefore, it was entirely out-of-date. Use your discretion, if you think it may be outdated or not relevant, don't include it. Remember you only have two pages!

Always put your highest/ most relevant qualifications at the top. If you have a degree/ professional qualification, those should go at the top, followed by others and then your work-based training.

Qualifications Gained Over 10 Years Ago

If you gained your qualifications over ten years ago, the dates/ grades/ school or college you attended are unnecessary, as they aren't relevant.

You also don't need to list each 'O'Level/ GCSE/ CSE/ 'A'Level title – just write 'O Levels' or 'GCSEs' etc., and the number of each gained. You may wish to add, *'including Maths and English'* if you have them.

You also don't need to list qualifications from other examining boards such as typing, shorthand, etc. as they will be out of date and don't add anything to an application.

Often, I find that clients with technical roles such as Health & Safety or positions that require a high level of training have numerous qualifications.   In these circumstances, it's perfectly acceptable to add an extra page just for them – it serves to highlight how qualified you are.

Top Tip - Avoid putting work-based training that isn't relevant to the roles that you're applying for (unless they're formal qualifications). They won't help you get the job, and you'll only be wasting valuable space.

SECTION 6 - ADDITIONAL INFORMATION

This section is entirely discretionary. A recruiter won't use it as a measurement; it simply gives a more holistic view of you. People are under the illusion that you have to include an 'Additional Information' section, e.g. hobbies and interests; you don't. You should only incorporate it if you have something to say that will enhance your application. For example, you should only list hobbies/ interests which align with company values. Interviewers like applicants who:

• Are involved with charities.

• Are involved in sports.

• Are involved with 'clubs' e.g. running/ painting/ football/ Scouts/ Guides/ Brownies/ Cadets, etc.

• Are studying – undertaking further education.

• Have a non-paid role in addition to their regular job, e.g. school governor, councillor, non-executive director.

• Are fluent in another language

TOP TIP - You should avoid the common hobbies/ interests that everyone *thinks* that they should write, e.g. cinema/ socialising/ reading/ gym. Everyone does those, and they say nothing about you. It would be better to leave this section out entirely if that's all you have to add, using the space to add more quality information elsewhere, e.g. additional achievements, rather than wasting space listing things that will not support your application.

If you do decide to include additional information:

- **Ensure that you can talk about it** - Whatever you write in this section must be current, i.e. *you must be doing it now*. I had one client who had written that he was a Scout leader, but when I quizzed him about it, he said that it five years ago, making it totally irrelevant now. People who *used* to have non-executive director roles or who *were* involved with charities find it especially difficult when I use my red pen to cross them, but if you're no longer doing something, it's not relevant. Anything you write here a prospective employer will assume that you're still doing, and it will seem odd to them if you aren't.

- **Tell the truth** – Don't put something if you don't do it. It's common for interviewers to explore anything you've listed in your 'additional information' in an interview. I've caught people lying when I've asked about their hobbies during an interview. I'll ask about the last film they watched if they listed 'cinema' as a hobby. I'm a massive film fan, and I know what's showing at the movies most of the time. If an interviewee can't answer me quickly or if they can't give me a recent film, I'll think they're lying.

That goes for 'reading' too. People like to list reading as a hobby, yet when I ask them what they're currently reading or who their favourite author/ genre is, they frequently can't answer.

Lying about your hobbies and interests and getting caught out will throw everything else you've said into question, which can mean that you fail an otherwise excellent interview.

OTHER ADDITIONAL INFORMATION

- **Clean driving license** – Only include this information if it's asked for in the advert/ job description/ person specification. These days it's assumed that most people drive and have access to a car.

You should **NOT** include any of the following:

- **Children/ marital status** – In the past, employers used this information in their decision-making process, e.g. more unscrupulous employers may not have wanted to employ women who had children because they may take too much time off work to look after them. Or they may have considered not recruiting single men as they might have believed them to be unreliable. It's now illegal to deselect a candidate using such criteria, and, therefore, recruiters prefer that you don't include it.

- **Nationality** – As long as you have the right documentation to be able to work in the UK, your nationality is irrelevant (although being able to speak English may be a prerequisite for a role).

- **Date of Birth** – As I've already mentioned, it's now illegal in the UK to discriminate on the grounds of age. Therefore, you do not need to include it on your CV.

- **Referees** – So many people write *'References available on request'* at the bottom of their CV. There's no need to state the obvious; it's a line that you can use for something more productive. You also don't need to waste space giving the names and contact details of your referees (unless explicitly asked for them) either. If you're successful at an interview, I'll guarantee that a good company will ask you for them as most job offers are conditional upon receiving two acceptable references. It's highly unlikely that they'll go back through your CV for the details.

- **Picture – ABSOLUTELY NOT!** In the UK, we don't use photographs on CVs. Recruiters don't like them due to the potential for discrimination, e.g. a candidate could claim that the company rejected their application because of their ethnicity, sex, age, etc. rather than their ability to do the job. Other countries are different; therefore, if you're applying for roles outside the UK, it would be a good idea to research the accepted photograph 'rule' for the country where the vacancy is based.

NOTE – Some companies have a blanket policy to reject any CVs which include any information which could be classed as discriminatory. For example, date of birth, marital status, nationality, photo, etc. to reduce the risk of litigation, i.e. a candidate may claim that they were discriminated against because that information was in their CV, and that's why they weren't invited to an interview.

SCHOOL/ UNIVERSITY/ COLLEGE LEAVERS

If you're a school/ college/ university graduate, it's unlikely that you'll have much relevant job information to include on a CV. Therefore, it's vital to embellish your other non-work-related achievements:

- If you've had a part-time job, you should naturally incorporate it into 'career history'. Explain what you did including your key responsibilities/ duties and what you achieved within that role (no matter how small). Include things like cash management, prioritisation, organisation, dealing with customers, relationship management, administration, etc.

- You must include an extended 'Additional Information' section, providing information on clubs and activities that you are involved with. Here are some examples of what you could incorporate:

  o Scouts/ Guides/ Cadets
  o Duke of Edinburgh Awards
  o Sports e.g. football/ netball/ hockey/ running etc.
  o Painting/ drawing/ design/ IT
  o Ballet/ dance/ drama/ arts
  o Working with young people or charities
  o Travelling
  o Languages you are fluent in

  This list is not exhaustive. Outline any achievements you've had in the course of your activities including qualifications, badges, certificates and a little around the key skills you needed to obtain them.

- You should also consider attaching a Personal Statement. A Personal Statement will give you the opportunity to tell the recruiter about the type of person you are, the skills and attributes that you have that make you suitable for their role and organisation.

TOP TIPS FOR COMPLETING YOUR CV

- Try to keep it to two pages of A4. However, initially, you could write a much longer CV containing everything you've done, editing it down to two pages based on the requirements for each individual application.

- If there is more than one type of job that you could apply for, consider writing two or three different CV's matching the skills/ experience required for each.

- Don't write 'CURRICULUM VITAE' at the top. Everyone knows what the document is and you only two pages, so don't waste the space.

- Write in the third person, i.e. do not use 'I,' 'me,' 'my,' 'mine,' 'we,' etc.

- Don't include your 'opinion,' e.g. hardworking, trustworthy, dedicated, etc. Everything you write should be factual and have evidence to back it up.

- Use typeface Arial pt 10 or 11 or Calibri pt. 11.

- If you have a professional role that requires many qualifications, list them on a separate page.

- Make sure your layout easy on the eye. Avoid tiny fonts and pushing content to the very edges of the page. Leave lots of white space.

- If printing paper, use quality paper.

- Check for typos, errors – ask someone else to check it. I recommend using a tool such as Grammarly (grammarly.com/) which you can use to correct grammar and spelling.

- Be truthful.

- **MAKE SURE IT'S ACHIEVEMENT FOCUSSED and ...**

- **TAILOR IT TO THE ROLE!**

Chapter 3 - Covering Letters

"The difference between something good and something great is attention to detail."

Covering letters are an essential part of the self-marketing process. It's your opportunity to sell yourself further, allowing you the chance to show a little more of your personality than you would in your CV. Therefore, if you have the option to attach a covering letter, you should always do it.

As part of my research, I met with a recruitment consultant friend of mine, and we were discussing the content of this book. He said, *"Jo, please put something in about covering letters. I can't tell you how frustrated I get when I receive a poor covering letter. I use the covering letter more than the CV now for pre-sifting – I sometimes don't even read the CV - so I get annoyed when it's poorly written."* He continued, *"Another bugbear is where the candidate has used a template, and they haven't edited it properly, sending it littered with mistakes. Also, I can't tell you how many times people get my name wrong, or shorten it. For goodness sake, if they can't even get my name right, well there's no way they're getting through to one of my clients, their application goes straight in the 'no' pile!"*

- Always write in the FIRST person – That means that you *can* include 'I,' 'me,' 'my,' 'we,' 'us.' However, minimise the use of the word 'we' as it implies that your achievements are as the result of a team effort rather than your own work.

- **Tailor it to the role**. Review the job description, person specification, and company's competencies (if possible) and adapt your letter to their requirements.

- Cut and paste from your CV where appropriate. Use your 'achievements', but do this sparingly; you don't want to replicate your entire CV!

- Be careful if you're overwriting an existing letter or using a template. You *must* double check that you've not made any mistakes and left any unwanted information from a previous application.

- Use your Power Words (as discussed in Chapter 3).

- Use typeface Arial pt. 10 or 11 or Calibri pt. 11.

- Keep it relatively short; the equivalent of one side of A4 paper.

- Make sure it's well laid out and easy on the eye.

- If printing hard copies, use quality paper.

- Check for typos, errors – ask someone else to check it.

- Tell the truth.

- If emailing your application, start with 'Dear Name' or 'Dear Sir/ Madam' and always end with, 'Kind regards' – DO NOT write, *"Hi"* even in an email.

- The correct endings if you're sending a paper copy or attaching a covering letter to an email:

  o Start with 'Dear Sir/ Madam' end with 'Yours faithfully.'

  o Start with 'Dear Name' end with 'Yours sincerely.'

- If you place the covering letter in the main body of an email, you should still start with 'Dear Name/ Sir/ Madam', but it's fine to end with, 'Kind regards'.

- Address the letter to the contact mentioned in the advert, where one there is one. Never shorten names and make sure that you get the recruiter's name right. If you don't, your application will usually get rejected straight away.

- Quote the job reference number (if applicable) and where you saw the role advertised.

- Use a polite and positive ending.

And I'll repeat it for emphasis - **MAKE SURE YOU TAILOR IT TO THE ROLE!**

Visit yourdreamjob.co.uk/ and sign up to receive two template copies of covering letters, including one for a specific vacancy, and one for speculative applications.

Chapter 4 - Application Forms

"Attention to detail will set you apart from competitors."

Apart from the traditional CV and covering letter, application forms are still a favourite pre-sifting tool for many recruiters. The past few years have seen significant developments in the way large organisations (who can receive literally hundreds of applications for a single vacancy) manage their recruitment. Many have now adopted automated processes, investing in computer software designed to handle bulk applications; this makes pre-sifting more efficient, and a lower cost option as it eliminates the need for human intervention in the first sift.

These programs will assess an application against specific essential criteria (keywords) for each position, e.g. qualifications, skills, experience, etc., usually taken for the job description or person specification. If a submission contains information that matches the requirements for the role, it will be highlighted, and reviewed further by a recruitment assessor. If not enough keywords can be found, it will automatically be rejected, potentially without ever being viewed by a human.

COMPLETING ONLINE APPLICATION FORMS

Online applications can be a little trickier to fill in than their paper counterparts. However, the following are guidance notes designed to ensure that you have the best chance of success.

1. **Print a copy before you start to fill it in online** – Where possible, print a copy and practise writing your answers before transferring them to the original online.

2. **Follow instructions carefully** – Many candidates tend to 'skim' read (usually, because they're nervous) and, therefore, don't give the correct answer or write too much/ too little information.

3. **Jot down ideas before you start** – By doing this, you'll lessen your chances of making errors.

4. **Confine answers to the space provided** – Unless you are told that you can use an extra sheet, you should adhere to the defined area, ensuring that your

answers are concise. I suggest you **use the achievements** that you've gathered for your CV and write them in the STAR format. The STAR format is covered in detail in Book 4 of the Your Dream Job series, 'Foolproof Interview Skills'.

a. **Situation** – What was the global, big company issue/ problem? This should be 10% of your overall answer.

b. **Task** – What was your role in solving that problem? This should be 10% of your overall answer.

c. **Action** – What action did you take in solving the problem? This should be 70% of your overall answer.

d. **Results** – What results did you achieve (include as many facts and figures as you can here, e.g. £, %, KPI increases/ decreases, etc. This should be 10% of your overall answer.

5. **Enter information accurately** - You should pay particular attention to dates, ensuring that they are correct. For some reason, candidates often mistype dates and forget to check them.

6. **Fill in ALL sections** - As application forms are often scored, if you skip a question you may be missing out on valuable points. Avoid jumping over parts thinking that you'll go back and fill in later, as you may forget, again potentially missing out on points.

7. **Stick to the number of words stipulated** – When there is a word count you should stick to it. Anything you write over and above will not receive a score. If you don't reach the word count, it's unlikely that you will have answered the question thoroughly enough to achieve top marks.

8. **Use the achievements from your CV** - If you are asked competency-based questions, e.g. *"Give an example of when you have had to ..."* use the 'achievements' that you have listed on your CV. Copy and paste them if appropriate (although you may need to add extra information – remember to use the recommended word count and write them using the STAR format). Where possible use the company's competencies to tailor your answers. Competencies are sometimes called 'values' or 'behaviours' and can often be found on a company's website. (Competencies are discussed in Book 4 of the Your Dream Job series, 'Foolproof Interview Skills'.)

9. **Check for typos/ errors** – We can't always see our own mistakes, therefore, ask someone else with a good command of written English to check it for you. I realise that this isn't always possible, especially if it's the kind of online form that won't let you go back once you've clicked 'NEXT.' If that's the case, take the time to carefully read each completed section out loud before clicking to the next page.

A way around this is to type your responses first in a word processing software program such as Microsoft Word or Apple's Pages, which will provide you with an accurate word count, as well as highlighting any spelling and grammatical errors. Once you are happy with what you've written, copy and paste your answers into the application form.

10. **Make sure that your referees know about your application and are happy to support you** – You will usually get asked for reference details on an application form. It's common courtesy to inform your referees that a prospective employer may contact them.

11. **Send it to the right person** – If the application process isn't automated, take care to email your application to the right person and that you have spelt their name and address/ email correctly.

12. **Complete it on time** – If your application is late, it will probably get rejected, no matter what your reason may be.

13. **Keep a copy** – This is important, as you'll need it to refer to it if you get selected for an interview. Sometimes with online application forms, you aren't able to go back once you've pressed enter. In this case, use the Print Screen button on your keyboard [PrtScn] and paste [Ctrl V] the screen print into MS Word, PowerPoint, Paint or an alternative software program.

    If you're using a Mac, hold down the 'cmd', 'shift' and number '4' buttons to select the area you want to copy. The highlighted area will automatically go to your desktop. It may be laborious, but it will be worth it.

    Another benefit of saving copies of completed application forms is that you can use the same information for subsequent applications, reducing re-work, saving time and energy.

HARD COPY APPLICATION FORMS

If you have a paper application form, make a copy of it and fill that in first. Once you're happy with your answers, transpose them onto the original. That way, you'll minimise the chance of making a mistake. Again, ask someone else to read and check it for errors and remember to keep a copy.

What Next?

"If it's important you'll find a way . . . if not, you'll find an excuse."

Keeping Up Momentum

It's easy to feel motivated in the first couple of weeks of a job search. Looking for the right job is front-loaded as there are more activities at the beginning, e.g. writing your CV, meeting recruitment consultants, joining websites, setting up your profile on LinkedIn and applying for numerous roles, etc. Once all those tasks have been completed, and job hunting turns into more of a maintenance function, it's fairly typical to hit a slump especially if you've received some rejections in the early days.

If this happens to you, it's worth revisiting the 'change curve' from Book 1 to remind yourself that negative feelings are completely natural. Reassure yourself that they won't last; it's just part of a process that you're going through; the most important thing is to keep going and not to get disheartened.

Here are my top tips related to the topics covered in this book:

1. **Get someone else to check your work –** No matter how good you think your written English skills are, we can't see our own mistakes. Ask someone with a good command of written English to review your CV/ covering letter/ application form.

   If that isn't possible, download an App such as Grammarly (grammarly.com/) to check your work – don't rely on your word processing package as they don't always pick up errors. You can download the basic version of Grammarly for free, and it will alert you to basic grammar and spelling mistakes that built-in spell checkers may not. It will also highlight where you've used the same word multiple times and offer you alternatives. If you have a PC, you can download the Grammarly MS Word add-on which allows you to check your work as you type. If you use a Mac, you can download the app and upload your completed documents for checking.

2. **Tailor your CV and covering letter to each new vacancy** – I realise that this can be tedious and time-

consuming, but it does pay dividends. You'll achieve far better results if you apply for a handful of roles using a tailored CV than you ever will using the same standard one for lots of different jobs using a scatter-gun approach.

3. **Update your CV on job sites** – Every week or, at least every two weeks, you should upload your CV to job websites again. Many recruiters enter date parameters when searching for candidates, looking for the most recent people to join the site or those who have recently updated their CV. Uploading a new one a minimum of every two weeks will mean that you will always remain at the top of searches.

4. **Tailor covering letters to the vacancy** – As with CVs, it's critical that you tailor covering letters to the job. However, unlike CVs, they should be written in the first person. Again, get someone to check it for typos if possible.

5. **Spell check application forms** – It's so easy to make mistakes on application forms. Wherever possible run your work through a spell checker before pressing submit on online applications.

6. **Keep copies** – I know I've mentioned this a number of times, but it's so important that you keep copies of CVs, covering letters, and application forms for when

you're invited to an interview. There's nothing worse than receiving an invitation, and you can't remember what CV/ covering letter you used or what you wrote on your application form.

FREQUENTLY ASKED QUESTIONS

Here is a selection of the most commonly asked questions from workshop delegates regarding topics covered in this book:

Q: I've worked for the same company for 20 years (although I've had various jobs in that time). Will a new employer see that as a negative?

It does depend on the recruiter; however, more importantly, it depends on how you position it. Some recruiters may view it as a negative, i.e. they may think that you only know one way of doing things or that you are set in your ways; however, it's up to you to demonstrate your versatility.

Research how things are done in other companies and review current industry/ profession best practice. This is where networking helps; if you know someone who does your role or a similar one in another company, call them and meet them for coffee. Get as much information from them as possible around techniques and practices used in their business. If you have had various positions, make sure that you can demonstrate your skills through your achievements in your previous roles too (particularly if they were less than 3-5 years ago) so that the recruiter can see your adaptability.

Rather than seeing your longevity as negative, many employers will view it as a positive as it indicates that you're loyal and are likely to stay with the company.

Q: I've had lots of jobs in the same company, how do I explain that on my CV?

Write the roles in the same way you would if they were external. Review Chapter 3 to understand how much information you should include within your current and previous positions. You only need to write the company name once with the 'start – present' dates, then detail each internal role together with the dates underneath.

Q: I've had lots of jobs in different companies, and I'm worried that employers will think that I have no staying power. What can I do about this?

First of all, you need to decide what you really want to do and the type of company you want to work for. The 'Get Clear' exercise described in Book 2 of the Your

Dream Job series, 'Finding Your Dream Job', is designed specifically for this purpose. Once you're clear about the job you want, revise your CV, tailoring it to those types of roles. You may wish to consider not including every job you've ever had as it could make your CV look too busy. Remove older positions, especially if they have no bearing on what you are applying for now.

If asked why you've had so many jobs, an excellent way to answer is to say that you've tried different things to establish what you really want to do. Explain that you've made a firm decision and are committed to finding and securing a job as an 'X.' However, be prepared to be able to explain the reasons for your choice.

Q: I've had a career gap – I went travelling/ took time off to look after my sick relative – how should I explain that on my CV?

Be truthful and write it on your CV as a career gap. Companies see travelling as a bonus as it shows that you're adventurous, you can work on your own initiative, that you're outgoing and actively seek out new opportunities. As for looking after a relative, no ethical company will have a problem with that as it shows a strength of character, caring nature, and loyalty.

If a company does have an issue with a career break, you have to consider whether it's a company you want to work for. Is there a possible 'values' clash?

Q: I've recently taken time out of work to raise my child/ children. How should I explain that on my CV?

I suggest that you write 'Career Break' and the dates. Remember that it's illegal for a company to discriminate against you for having children.

Q: I've been out of work for a while, will that look bad to a prospective employer?

Increasingly people are taking 'time out' after being made redundant. For most, it's the first time in their careers that have the opportunity to take significant time off work legitimately. Many decide to go travelling, carry out work in the house, spend time with their family, and that's perfectly fine. Most employers won't have a problem with that, and if they do, again you have to ask yourself if that's the type of company for whom you wish to work. It's a more palatable way to explain periods of unemployment, rather than saying that you couldn't find a job.

Q: I've been in interim roles for the last few years, and now I want a permanent job. Do you think I'll have a problem getting a permanent position?

It's likely that a company will be concerned that you might not stay in a permanent role. You might have to convince them that you want to settle down and that theirs is the right job/ company for you. To do this, consider telling them that you've enjoyed your time gaining a wealth of experience that you wouldn't have been able to acquire in just one company.

Q: You say that I need to keep my CV to two pages. However, I've got experience in lots of different areas, and I want the employer to know about it. Why can't I include it?

Your CV is your primary marketing tool – the document that will hopefully get you an interview. Therefore, it should only contain information that backs up your skills and experience that corresponds to the requirements of the vacancy. Everything else will be viewed as 'noise', and won't help you to secure an interview. Save your other great skills, achievements and experience to discuss when you meet the recruiter.

Additional Resources

Visit yourdreamjob.co.uk/ and sign up to receive the following documents explicitly designed to complement the content of the 'Your Dream Job' series, straight to your inbox:

- 'Get Clear' Template

- Power Words

- CV Template

- Contact Spreadsheet - Networking

- Contact Spreadsheet – Recruitment Consultants/ Agencies

- Job Application Tracker

- Daily Action Plan

- Covering Letter 1 – Speculative Applications

- Covering Letter 2 – Specific Applications

- Letter of Resignation

You can also join the dedicated Your Dream Job Facebook group:

facebook.com/YDJYourDreamJob/

Your Dream Job Online

Following the success of my corporate career management programmes and the full, 'Land Your Dream Job Now!' book, I have designed the Your Dream Job online programme. It provides step by step instructions and guidance on everything you need to know to find and land Your Dream Job. It is packed full of tried and tested, easy to use tools and techniques gained from working with thousands of job hunters, recruitment consultants, and internal recruiters/assessors, as well as experience from the thousands of new employees I've recruited during my career.

WHAT'S INCLUDED IN THIS PROGRAMME?

There are three individual courses included in the programme. You can either purchase the programme in its entirety or buy each individual course as needed. For more information on the full programme, visit: https://what-next.teachable.com/p/your-dream-job

WRITE A BRILLIANT CV

Write a brilliant CV teaches you how to write a succinct, achievement based, tailored CV using a set template which has been proven to achieve results thousands of times. I will show you what to and what not to include, how to best utilise space and most importantly and how to tailor your CV to a specific vacancy, giving you the best chance of being selected for an interview. For full details of this course visit:

https://what-next.teachable.com/p/your-dream-job-cv/.

Finding Your Dream Job

Many job seekers, unfortunately, give up their hunt before finding their dream job, usually because can't seem to find the right role (typically because their search isn't extensive enough), or, they don't get the results they were hoping for and struggle to maintain their enthusiasm. The Finding Your Dream Job course is specifically designed to give you a comprehensive list of vacancy sources and how to get the best out of them, together with how to manage your job hunt so that you maintain your motivation, massively increasing your chances of finding the right job for you. For full details of this course visit:

https://what-next.teachable.com/p/your-dream-job-search/

Foolproof Interview Skills

Most people don't realise, but **YOU CAN PREPARE FOR 85% OF ANY INTERVIEW**, and in this course, you will learn how. Foolproof Interview Skills provides you with everything you need to know to succeed at even the toughest of interviews. It contains comprehensive instructions on how and what to prepare as well as how to answer most general interview questions using a specific, easy to follow formula. In addition, you will learn how to answer the Top Ten Most Asked Interview Questions. I've also included a section focusing solely on what to expect on the day, including how to overcome interview nerves and how to perform at your optimum level, putting you streets ahead of your competitors. For full details of this course visit:

https://what-next.teachable.com/p/your-dream-job-interview-skills/

WHAT NEXT ONLINE SCHOOL

To join the 'What Next' online school for updates on upcoming online training, visit:

https://what-next.teachable.com

Reference Links

For more information on the services that What Next Consultancy (UK) Ltd provides (including one-to-one transformational and career coaching with Jo herself) and to read testimonials about how her coaching has helped her clients visit:

www.whatnextconsultancy.co.uk

You can also sign up for the What Next Newsletter, a monthly email which includes hints and tips for leading a healthier, more productive and happier life. You can also keep up-to-date with Jo's most recent tips and advice by reading her blog at:

www.whatnextconsultancy.co.uk/blog

Jo also has her own website at:

www.jobanks.net

Employment Law Advice: ACAS

www.acas.org.uk

Helpline 0300 123 1100

Right to Work documentation:

www.gov.uk

Job Centre Plus:

www.direct.gov.uk/en/Employment/Jobseekers/

Citizen's Advice Bureau:

www.citizensadvice.org.uk/

Recruitment Agencies/Consultancies and Online Job Sites:

- www.totaljobs.com
- www.reed.co.uk
- www.indeed.co.uk
- www.monster.co.uk
- www.jobsite.co.uk
- www.pertemps.co.uk
- www.glassdoor.co.uk
- www.michaelpage.co.uk
- www.hays.co.uk
- www.roberthalf.co.uk
- www.pertemps.co.uk
- www.manpower.co.uk
- www.reed.co.uk
- www.bluearrow.co.uk
- www.adecco.co.uk

About the Author

Jo Banks, a Business Owner, Author, Transformational Coach, NLP Master Practitioner, CBT Therapist and author, has more than 20 years' experience as a Senior HR Professional, establishing her own Coaching and Consultancy Practice, What Next Consultancy (UK) Ltd in 2009. With knowledge of working within a range of industries, Jo has a strong track record in positively creating high-performance cultures and dealing with complex people issues.

Jo is passionate about helping individuals and organisations to reach their full potential, through her proven and innovative coaching style. While she has trained in the traditional coaching methods, through coaching approximately 1500 people, Jo has found her own unique style focusing on behavioural change and fundamentally changing clients' thought patterns to achieve tangible results, super-charging their performance and elevating their career or business to the next level.

Jo runs inspirational leadership development stand-alone workshops, which include conflict management, communication skills, effective leadership, team development, advanced influencing and communication skills. She has also developed year-long Leadership Programmes which incorporate revolutionary workshops backing up the learning with one-to-one coaching. All Jo's work focuses predominantly on challenging thoughts and perceptions providing a unique blend of information and practical techniques that can put into practice immediately.

As well as providing coaching and leadership development, Jo has developed innovative Outplacement and Redeployment programmes which she and her colleagues deliver to organisations experiencing organisational change. She has combined her knowledge of recruitment (gained from interviewing thousands of people throughout her HR career), plus her insider knowledge of the recruitment industry, with her unique style of coaching to design unique programmes that deliver exceptional results.

'Land Your Dream Job Now!' is Jo's second book and describes the very best of her career management techniques. It provides easy to follow guidelines designed to enhance personal effectiveness in putting

readers streets ahead of their competitors, enabling them to *'Land Their Dream Job.'*

Jo's first book *'Thoughts Become Things: Change Your Thoughts Change Your World'* is also available at Amazon. It centres on the principles that she uses in her unique style of coaching. It is geared towards changing thoughts and behaviours by providing tools and techniques to understand ourselves and others better, to achieve exceptional results.

CONNECT WITH JO

Twitter: @JoBanks247

LinkedIn: jo-banks-738b4412

Facebook: jobanks.net/

Instagram: Jobanks247

Web 1: jobanks.net

Web 2: yourdreamjob.co.uk

Web 3: whatnextconsultancy.co.uk

Web 4: thoughtsbecomethings.co.uk

Blog: yourdreamjob.co.uk/blog

jobanks.net/blog

'Thoughts Become Things'

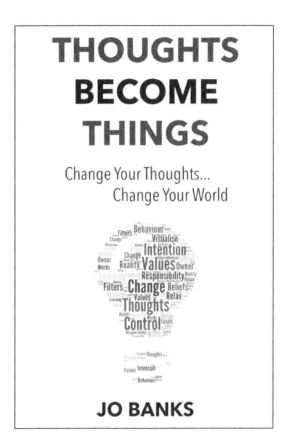

'Thoughts Become Things: Change Your Thoughts Change Your World' is available now, worldwide from Amazon in both Kindle and paperback versions. For more information visit:

thoughtsbecomethings.co.uk/

Printed in Great Britain
by Amazon